UNSETTLED

THE 100 YEAR WAR OF RESISTANCE BY XHOSA AGAINST BOER AND BRITISH

CEDRIC NUNN

Pirogue

First published as *Unsettled: The 100 Years War of Resistance by Xhosa Against Boer and British* by the Pirogue Collective, Brooklyn, New York, 2015

Pirogue Collective / Island Position
c/o Archipelago Books
232 3rd Street #A111
Brooklyn, NY 11215

Library of Congress Cataloging-in-Publication Data
Nunn, Cedric.
Unsettled: The 100 Years War of Resistance by Xhosa Against Boer and British / Cedric Nunn – First Island Position edition.
pages ; cm
ISBN 978-0-914671-44-2
I. Title

Cover photograph: Cedric Nunn

Book design: Peter Holm, Sterling Hill Productions

PRINTED IN THE UNITED STATES OF AMERICA

In remembrance and honour of the many
ancestors who fell in defense of our freedom.

PREFACE

*"The discovery of America, and that of passage to the East Indies
by the Cape of Good Hope, are the two greatest and most important events recorded in the History of mankind."*

Adam Smith, *The Wealth Of Nations*

The South African landscape is drenched in blood. From the time of its inception when the coast was navigated by European nations – Portuguese, Dutch, French and English – repeated violence has been visited upon its inhabitants. At first, the Cape was seen as simply a refreshment station by the various marine enterprises. Later it was understood that the port played a vital role in controlling the trade route on which it lay.

It became increasingly clear that to occupy the Cape meant being involved in the interior, and indeed occupying that as well. So, after the violent settling of the Cape and the rapid expansion of settlers into the interior, these clashes, which resulted in genocide against the San and Khoi, were encountered by the Xhosa of the now eastern Cape. This clash of civilizations was to result in an armed conflict lasting one hundred years.

From 1779 to 1879 the Xhosa people were subjected to nine wars of aggression, first by Afrikaner settlers and then British colonial and settler forces intent on conquering their territory.

The enormity of this event is still seemingly lost on South Africans. In our popular imagination we see the Zulu as the epitome of the African warrior, when it is the

San, the Khoi, and particularly the Xhosa that are more deserving of the title. Any nation that could stave off the admittedly superior arms technology of the British for a period of one hundred years deserves recognition.

The horrors that were inflicted on these brave patriots who fiercely resisted domination are almost unimaginable to us today. The tactics such as scorched earth policies, banishments, massacres, and divisionary strategies that they experienced would go on to be employed throughout the dominated regions of empire.

This essay looks at the land, which was occupied, desired, defended, lost, and won. In it we see its current uses and conditions, both for the victors and the vanquished. We are able to imagine the heroism and misery of its population as people chose to either defend or attack. We see, too, how little of this memory is commemorated or honoured. We see the smug conquerors and their victims. We see the continuing collaborations, which have always been necessary to maintain the status quo. We see the beauty, which stirred the souls of the inhabitants and the lust of the invaders.

Through revisiting this painful past in the contemporary scenes of today, this work attempts to place the present in its factual context of dispossession and conquest. We begin to understand the troubled nature of a people vanquished through open warfare and every divisionary trick in the book.

— Cedric Nunn, 2014

FOREWORD

A Storage Place of Memory

These landscapes are storage places of memory. Embedded in the nooks and crannies of these rocks, these dongas, these trees, these hills, these rivers, these valleys, these ruins, these monuments, these cities, these cairns . . . are generations of narratives that continue to haunt the present. Behind each image rendered in monochrome by Cedric Nunn's sensitive lenses – sometimes in a sullen mood, at other times in a serene one, and again at some moments in a deadpan manner – lurks tales of heroism and villainy, of romance and betrayal. Among these deep shadows speckled with moments of delicate light walk centuries of prophets, freedom fighters, lovers and traitors.

War is predominant in the memory-vaults of these landscapes. Contemporary farmlands with modern irrigation systems were once the fertile lands that lured the colonist settlers to the territories of amaXhosa resulting in The One Hundred Years War of Resistance – historians, of course, like to round up figures neatly; these were a series of many so-called "Frontier Wars" that lasted for far more than a hundred years. Despite the evocation of solitude in Nunn's photographs, those rivers and those hills recall the chants and the screams that resounded to the heavens when those farmlands were nothing more than theatres of war – villages and fields and grazing lands, all property owned by amaXhosa that had to be defended against colonial encroachment.

Right from the beginning land was at the center of European conquest and African resistance, both as the stage where these bloody performances were taking place and as the prize – the bounty that the victorious took possession of. No wonder it is the land that dominates these photographs, images that evoke footprints of The One Hundred Years War of Resistance. It is the land that is custodial to memory. Nunn's land is sometimes scarred and bleeding with dongas cutting mercilessly through it. But quite often it is lush with rivers and aloes and bushes and rich farmlands. Hills carved like calves in grainy grey against the horizon.

Very few human figures. Descendants of the actors of yesteryear and their mangy dogs and their goats in dilapidated villages or in church or in forlorn soccer fields. Progeny of Makhanda and Ntsikana and Mhlakaza and Maqoma and Mhlontlo and Ngqika and Ndlambe. Ndlambe! The name reverberates over and over through the images – be they place-names, descendants, or memorials of battlefields such as Amalinde.

He lives in memory as the regent-king of amaRharhabe who led his people in many battles against colonial forces in the early years of The One Hundred Years, in what is featured in historical records as the Cape-Xhosa Wars of 1811–19. For a while he made his stand against the alliances of the British, the Boer and the Khoikhoi forces who were deployed along the Sunday River and determined to push him across the Fish River. Ultimately his forces folded when the enemy indiscriminately massacred women and children of the amaRharhabe people and their amaGqunukhwebe allies.

But his biggest rival, even more than the British, was his own nephew, the rightful heir to the throne of amaRharhabe, Ngqika. Did I say rival? They were sworn enemies. Their conflict amounted to a civil war, each side with its ardent followers, its own military forces, and its own spiritual leaders and prophets. Under Ngqika's patronage was the great prophet Ntsikana, reputed to be the first Christian convert among amaXhosa. He preached peaceful co-existence with white colonists. On Ndlambe's side was another great prophet, Nxele, who is reputed to have prophesied the coming of the white man long before his advent, and urged that amaXhosa should drive the whites into the sea.

Nxele (also known as Makana or Makhanda) was so much of a thorn in the side of the colonist that they sentenced him to life imprisonment on Robben Island where he drowned trying to escape. To this day his followers are waiting for his return, and he lives in an isiXhosa proverb: *ulindele ukuza kukaNxele* – you are waiting for the return of Nxele. We say this when you are waiting for something that will never happen. Like when we were waiting for Nelson Mandela to be released from prison during the days of apartheid. Kaiser Matanzima, his uncle, and the president of the Bantustan Republic of the Transkei would warn us, "You are waiting for the return of Nxele!"

These landscapes are storage places of memory. These are not pretty, clichéd images of romantic sunsets of the Eastern Cape. They are indeed lacking in grandiosity. Yet in their understated beauty and their seemingly mundane subjects, their intensified composition expresses more than what we see on the surface. They are aesthetically pleasing in their own right even without the memories of romance, lust, and betrayal embedded in them.

Talking of lust and romance and betrayal: the woman's name was Thuthula. She was famous for her beauty and she was one of Ndlambe's young wives. Ngqika lusted after her and therefore abducted her from Ndlambe's seraglio. This had serious consequences for Ngqika. Many of his followers deserted him as they regarded this as an act of incest, sleeping with his own aunt. But Thuthula, who claimed to have been in a loveless marriage as Ndlambe's eleventh wife, had fallen deeply in love with Ngqika and stayed with him even after he had been impoverished as a result of the elopement and the flight of his subjects and subsidiary chiefs. Twenty years later Europeans who visited Ngqika's court, now recovered from destitution, wrote of the legendary Thuthula, of how tall, beautiful, and graceful she continued to be, how her behavior (note *her* behavior, not Ngqika's) caused greater scandal and more bad blood than any other woman's behavior in the history of the amaXhosa, and how after all those years she continued to wield so much influence over Ngqika and was obviously the power behind Ngqika's throne.

Subsequent generations have been inspired to write songs and poems about Thuthula. James J R Jolobe has his famous isiXhosa poem about her, translated by his own hand into turgid English. Inspired by this poem, an Eastern Cape playwright, Chris Zith-ulele Mann, wrote a play "Thuthula – Heart of the Labyrinth," which was performed at the 2003 National Arts Festival in Grahamstown.

These landscapes are storage places of memory but memory can be contentious. Chris Mann's play became very controversial, not because anyone contested the content but rather through the very act of remembering. The question becomes: why remember, and why bring these memories to the attention of others and force them to remember too? This was the position of the traditional leaders of the Eastern Cape, partic-ularly Maxhoba Sandile, the king of the amaRharhabe people and direct descendant of Ngqika and Ndlambe. He called a meeting of all the chiefs in his jurisdiction and lashed out at the playwright and the director, Janet Buckland, for failing to consult the king before composing the play. As if these artists lived in some feudal state where freedom of expression was non-existent and artistic composition was by fiat. The king's representative, Prince Zolile Burns-Ncamashe, threatened a court interdict because the monarchy had been disrespected and embarrassed by exposing ancient stories that caused the disunity of the amaXhosa people. Their main gripe about the play was that "it will bring back sad memories of the tragic past."

The play was, of course, performed.

It emerged during that uproar that some young women looked at Thuthula as a feminist hero because, as writer Yolisa Madola said, she was the first woman to stand up against male dominance in the society of amaXhosa.

On these black and white landscapes have walked even more powerful women. A few years before Thuthula was born, in the northern part of the Eastern Cape, Phahlo, the king of the amaMpondomise people was dying. His senior wife only had daughters, and according to custom the heir could only be male and therefore would have to come from the junior wives. But Mamani, the first-born from the senior wife insisted that she was the rightful heir and would take the throne even though she was female. This was unheard of and the elders of amaMpondomise put their collective foot down; it would not happen. Mamani was headstrong. She was the first-born. There was no reason she would not be heir. She armed herself and brutally killed anyone who opposed her. In no time the military fell in her command and the elders toed the line. Mamani became the king of amaMpondomise. When the time came for Mamani to marry, she surprised everyone by insisting that she would marry a woman. She sent emissaries to the land of amaMpondo to ask for Ntsibatha's hand, who was Nyawuza's daughter. This was the first officially-sanctioned same-sex marriage known in what later became South Africa. And indeed there was an heir to the throne, Mngcambe, Ntsibatha's son conceived with one of Mamani's brothers.

Today no Mpondomise man worth his macho salt wants to remember Mamani. This amnesia can be heard when the royal elders recite their genealogy: they start with Sibiside who led abaMbo from the Great Lakes circa 1400, followed by a litany of names, and then from Phahlo they jump straight to Mngcambe, skipping Mamani as if she never existed. It is a shameful memory, except for pesky artists like me – Mamani features quite prominently in the novel I am currently writing titled *Little Suns*. I hope I am not going to have traditional leaders of all sorts raising

Cain for my writing about a shameful episode in their history – which, by the way, is my history.

Mamani's great-grandson was Mhlontlo, the last king of amaMpondomise who was exiled in Lesotho from 1882 to 1903 after the killing of the magistrate Hamilton Hope. His resistance against British forces and their amaMfengu and amaMpondo allies in 1880 was really the final war in The One Hundred Years War of Resistance. It is his story that I tell in *Little Suns*.

The memories stored in Nunn's images have been the subject of many more breathtaking art forms. The fairy-tale melancholia of his Balfour/Kat River/Winterberg photography, the landscape being the former seat of Chief Maqoma, reminded me of the most trance-inducing dance performance I have seen in recent years. It was in July 2014 at the American Dance Festival in Durham, North Carolina, and the dancer was Gregory Vuyani Maqoma in a piece titled *Exit/Exist*. Here the dancer revisits ancestral memory, how the warrior Chief Maqoma fought colonial dispossession, lost his cattle, and was confined to Robben Island where he died in 1873, aged 75. The dancer embodies this history in a transformational and poignant performance fusing narrative with spirited performance modes accompanied by harmonies and anguished lamentations by a four-man South African vocal ensemble.

Similarly, the dramatic contrasts and luminous tonality of Nunn's Nongqawuse images, be they portrayals of the prophetess's burial place or memorials of cattle killings or sites of resistance, cannot but remind us of the plethora of creative works surrounding these events. The age of Nxele and Ntsikana taught us that the Eastern Cape has always been a fertile ground for prophets and prophesies. In the mid-1850s among the amaGcaleka people, the most celebrated were Nongqawuse and Nonkosi, both teenagers who led a millennialist movement that culminated in the mass killing of cattle by amaXhosa. Nongqawuse and her friend Nombanda, later joined by Nonkosi, preached that they had received instructions from the spirits of the ancestors that the people must kill all their animals and destroy all their crops, for they were all infected by *ubuthi* – witch-craft. On a particular day the ancestor would arise from the dead and come with new disease-free cattle, and the fields would be flush with new crops. Most importantly a great storm would come and drive all the white people to the sea and amaXhosa would live in freedom once again. Many amaXhosa bought into the prophecies and killed their cattle and destroyed their crops. They were called the Believers (Amathamba). However, there were some who refused to kill their cattle; they did not believe the prophecies. They were called the Unbelievers (Amagogotya). A civil war broke out between the two groups. The day came, the dead did not arise. Great famine followed and many people perished. This was dubbed The Great Xhosa Mass Suicide and to this day many amaXhosa people believe that Sir George Grey had a hand in Nongqawuse's prophecies.

Songs have been composed about Nongqawuse, the daughter of Mhlakaza (she was actually Mhlakaza's ward, some say niece). A 1935 play by H I E Dhlomo "The Girl Who Killed to Save: Nongqawuse the Liberator" seemed to suggest that the cattle-killing episode was liberatory in that it hastened the adoption of Christianity by the "Xhosa national soil-soul" and the propagation of law and order, science, medicine, and education. An earlier national poet, S E K Mqhayi, wrote of Nongqawuse as a dupe of British missionaries and colonial officials. The painter George Pemba portrayed her in a 1987 painting as a dignified young woman. I, on the other hand, portrayed her in my novel *The Heart of Redness* as a true believer. Inkosi Phathekile Holomisa of the abaThembu people once asked me, "Why do you people keep on writing about Nongqawuse? What are you teaching our children? This is not an episode of our history that we want to remember."

Exactly. Contested memory as always. A demand for amnesia where it suits a certain class of people.

It reminded me of some amaGcaleka elders that I met in Centani who felt very aggrieved that I was writing about Nongqawuse. This is a story that must be forgotten, they insisted, for it portrays our ancestors in a very bad light. It shows how stupid they were to be deceived by young girls, resulting in so many deaths. Again the notion that there is "good history" and there is "bad history". Students must only learn "good history." "Bad history" must be buried once and for all.

Long after The One Hundred Years War of Resistance these black and white terrains with shades of grey continue to be haunted by prophets who walked side-by-side with freedom fighters. Thankfully the memorialized Steve Biko. Thankfully the memorialized Settlers and Trekboers. Many others unsung and unmemorialized. These landscapes are storage places of their memory, too.

— Zakes Mda

INTRODUCTION

The One Hundred Years War (1779-1878) between Colonist and Xhosa on the Cape's Eastern Frontier was not only South Africa's most protracted anti-colonial confrontation, but also one of its most complex. Just as every coin has two sides, so every historical interaction has two faces: the settlement of one community implies the destabilisation of the other, the resistance of the latter derails the progress of the former. This historical process leaves neither side untouched: they understand each other better but they also misunderstand each other more; they come ever closer together but they never quite meet. Historical relationships in the Eastern Cape were, moreover, triangular rather than bilateral: more flexible than either Colonist or Xhosa, the Khoisan community was vulnerable to both.

The images in this collection capture the nuances of Eastern Cape history better than words can ever do, but the following brief summary of that history may help to contextualize them in space and time.

Thanks to the journal of the Beutler expedition (Crampton 2013), we know for certain that the easternmost point of Dutch settlement in 1752 was Mossel Bay, and the westernmost point of Xhosa settlement was the Fish River. The lands between were occupied by a variety of Khoisan entities, including the warlike Oeswana

San, the remnants of the Inqua kingdom of the Camdeboo, and the chiefdom of an escaped murderer named Ruiter, who had established himself in the so-called Zuurveld, which is the present day district of Grahamstown. By the time Governor Van Plettenberg concluded a botched treaty with some minor Xhosa chiefs in 1778 (Peires 2008), Khoisan independence was irrevocably lost. In 1779, the First Frontier War broke out in the present district of Somerset East, known to the trekboers as Boschberg and the Xhosa as Nojoli. The Colonists won that round but were unable to maintain their position, and the Second (1793) and Third (1799–1803) Wars must count as Xhosa victories.

In 1806, the British took over the government of the Cape, and completely altered the balance of forces on the Cape Eastern Frontier. During the Fourth Frontier War (1811–2), by the judicious application of "a proper degree of terror," Colonel John Graham drove the Xhosa across the Fish River and established the City of Grahamstown as the military and political centre of the Eastern Cape (Fourth Frontier War 1811–2). The Xhosa attempt to recover their territory culminated in the Battle of Grahamstown (Fifth Frontier War 1818–9), when the sources of the Kowie River ran so red with Xhosa blood that the Kowie ditch, separating white Grahamstown from black Grahamstown during the apartheid era, is known as "Egazini" ("place of blood") to the present day.

The British followed up their victory of 1819 with the introduction of 5,000 British immigrants to settle the hitherto contested Zuurveld. The harbour settlement at Algoa Bay was renamed Port Elizabeth in honour of the recently deceased wife of Acting Governor Sir Rufane Donkin. As the British moved in, most Eastern Cape Afrikaners moved out in what became known as the "Great Trek" (1838). The lands they vacated, in Graaff-Reinet for instance, were taken over by enterprising British farmers who introduced merino sheep and initiated economic developments in the Bay area which soon caused Port Elizabeth to eclipse Grahamstown and rival Cape Town itself.

Meanwhile the colonial frontier pushed forward in a series of three Frontier Wars, each more bloody than the one before: the Sixth Frontier War, known as Hintsa's War (1834–5), the Seventh Frontier War, known as the War of the Axe (1846–7) and the Eighth Frontier War, known as the War of Mlanjeni (1850–3). This is not the place to relate the story of these wars, which may be found in Milton (1983), Mostert (1992) and, for a Xhosa version, Mqhayi (2009). The dark record of atrocities on both sides was only occasionally alleviated by such incidents as occurred at Salem when the unarmed pacifist Richard Gush saved the settler village by offering its Xhosa attackers a gift of bread and tobacco (Butler 1982). The Xhosa fought guerrilla style in the forests and mountains, avoiding open combat. Pitched battles, such as the Battle of the Gwangqa (June 1846) happened only rarely, and always resulted in mass slaughter by the armed and mounted British forces. Unable to fight in the bush themselves, the British depended on Khoisan and Mfengu auxiliaries. Mostly, however, they took their time, destroyed the enemy maizefields, and starved the Xhosa out in a war of attrition. By the end of the Eighth Frontier War (1853), the military situation remained deadlocked. The Xhosa were unable to drive out the British, but the British were equally unable to defeat the Xhosa.

Before proceeding , however, it is necessary to go back in time and consider the social and spiritual impact of the colonial intrusion. Politically, the colonial Governors were very adept at "divide and rule," that is, exploiting tensions between Xhosa chiefs such as Ngqika (d. 1829) and his uncle Ndlambe (d. 1828). But far more profound divisions occurred as a result of the introduction of Christianity. The first and, in some ways, the most important of the missionaries, was Dr J T Van der Kemp, a Dutch medical doctor working for the London Missionary Society. Van der Kemp was a true zealot who never confused the Christian religion with European-style civilisation. He made a point of living as simply as possible, and his teaching was "of a conversational character," sitting under a tree and talking about God (Wauchope 2008). He soon evoked the ire of the colonial authorities, who harried him from place to place, but the Xhosa called him uNyengane, "the one who gives secretly," implying that he had left his own people, the whites, to give precious information to the blacks.

Van der Kemp's teachings were appropriated in very different ways by two of the most towering figures in Xhosa intellectual history: Ntsikana, the Christian prophet, and Nxele Makhanda. Ntsikana prophesied that men with hair like cow's tails (whites) would come to Xhosaland, bringing the Word but also bringing "buttons without holes" (money). Take the Word, he advised the people, but leave the money alone. Nxele's teaching was very different. The white people, he said, had killed the son of God (Jesus), and God had punished them by throwing them into the sea out of which they had crawled to plague the black people. Nxele led the attack on Grahamstown in 1819 and was imprisoned on Robben island, where he drowned trying to escape.

Christian teachings also impacted greatly on the Eastern Cape Khoisan who had merged with ex-slaves, mulattoes, and some deracialised whites to create an entirely new Afri-kaans-speaking community, generally known in South Africa as "coloureds" as distinct from isiXhosa speaking Africans. Reduced to landlessness, they found their only refuge on such mission stations as Bethelsdorp, established by Van der Kemp in 1802. In 1829, the Kat River settlement (later known as the district of Stockenstrom), was established for their exclusive occupation. As Christians, they felt it their duty to support the Christian British government against the heathen Xhosa. They fought bravely and effectively as colonial auxiliaries during the Sixth and Seventh Frontier Wars, but incurred the enmity of the extreme settler element, who wished to tie them down as forced labour on the settler farms. When, therefore, the Eighth Frontier War broke out in 1850, some Kat River soldiers mutinied and seized Fort Armstrong in the Kat River valley. The rebellion spread to other Eastern Cape mission stations, especially Theopolis near Port Alfred, which was burned down in retaliation by the colonial forces. The Kat River rebels joined the Xhosa Chief Maqoma in the Waterkloof mountains (Adelaide district), which they occupied for over eighteen months in defiance of the entire British army. They were great readers of the Bible, and truly believed that the day of their deliverance was at hand. As Willem Uithaalder, their leader, put it, "Trust therefore in the Lord . . . for now is the time, yea, the appointed time, and no other."

Similar expectations of divine intervention had been circulating among the Xhosa since the days of Dr Van der Kemp. Prior to the battle of Grahamstown, Nxele Makhanda had summoned his followers to Gompo (Cove Rock) near East London to witness the damnation of the witches and the rising of the dead. Long after he was drowned, many Xhosa still believed he would return and, in 1850, his spirit was manifested in Mlanjeni, the riverman, who doctored the Xhosa army for the Eighth Frontier War. Mlanjeni's charms failed to protect the Xhosa warriors against colonial bullets, but he seemed to perform a number of miracles, sinking the troopship *Birkenhead* in February 1852 with the loss of 491 British soldiers. Before Mlanjeni died, he predicted the imminent coming of the expected redeemer, Sifuba-sibanzi (the broad-chested one), a figure first visualised in the prophecies of Ntsikana.

One fateful day in April 1856, Sifuba-sibanzi appeared to the teenage girl Nongqawuse, as she stood in her uncle's fields near the mouth of the River Kei. Xhosa cattle were dying in great numbers due to bovine lungsickness, a European import. Sifuba-sibanzi told Nongqawuse that the Xhosa cattle and crops had been contaminated by the sins of the people, that they must purify themselves, destroy all their possessions, and prepare the world for a fresh start. The blind would see, the deaf would hear, new cattle and corn would fill the kraals and grainpits, the dead would arise and no one would ever again lead a troubled life. 400,000 cattle were killed over a period of eighteen months but the predictions remained unfulfilled. Thousands of starving people converged on King William's Town where the apparently liberal Governor Sir

George Grey had prepared famine relief – on condition of the destitute signing up for contract labour. Many never made it, and their bodies were buried in a mass grave which has only recently been identified. Nongqawuse herself was taken to Cape Town by order of Sir George Grey, and most Xhosa today believe that she was his ignorant tool. She returned under an assumed name, and spent her remaining years on a farm in the district of Alexandria. After Sandile, the last Xhosa king, perished in the desperate but hopeless Ninth Frontier War/War of Ngcayechibi (1877–8), the remaining lands of the independent Xhosa kingdom west of the Kei were given out to the next generation of settlers.

Meanwhile, Sir George Grey pursued his policy of integrating white and black by assimilating Xhosa-speaking people into British Victorian culture. To this end, he sponsored mission schools such as Healdtown to provide industrial education for black artisans. He eliminated the Xhosa chiefs as a political force, sending many of them to Robben Island, but facilitated the emergence of a peasant class, composed of *amagogotya* (black people who had refused to kill their cattle) and colonial auxiliaries. He allocated land to his clients checkerboard style – small black farms alongside bigger white farms – in the hope that the different communities would learn from each other. These arrangements gave the Eastern Cape west of the Kei River, a political and social character entirely distinct from the lands across the Kei ("the Transkei") which colonialism swallowed whole twenty years later, leaving their precolonial socio-economic structures somewhat more intact.

The destructive edge of Sir George Grey's policies worked only too well. His more constructive policies were all in vain. Peasant agriculture boomed and the mission schools flourished, but only for a short time as the transformations wrought by the mineral revolution of the 1880s closed down the space for small producers, and left Xhosa people with few opportunities besides migrant labour. Grey's vision of black

English and white English living side by side, motivated by a single ideal and governed by a common law, fell victim to the rising tide of racial segregation after white South Africa united in 1910. In 1928, Grey's motley collection of isolated black landholdings were administratively combined under the title of the Ciskei Territorial Authority. The old intellectual tradition, which had culminated with the establishment of Fort Hare University at Alice, was deprived of its original social base and sense of purpose, and naturally inclined to national issues and more radical politics. In the rural areas, inter-racial and mutually advantageous arrangements like share-cropping (white landowner, black workforce, profit-sharing rather than wage labour) were disallowed and displaced black peasants drifted into places like Duncan Village, unemployed and discontented.

Alert to the political, though not the humanitarian, implications of their policies, and encouraged by the seeming success of the Matanzima government in Transkei, the South African government embarked around 1970 on the ambitious project of creating a Ciskei homeland that would replace the failed schemes of Sir George Grey. First and foremost, the apartheid planners deemed it necessary to consolidate "Ciskei" as a geographical entity. This meant expropriating vast tracts of white-owned land in districts such as Peddie and Whittlesea and populating them with the residents of "awkwardly situated Bantu areas" (also known as "black spots") in a sort of exchange. Historic German settler villages such as Frankfort and Hamburg were eliminated and valuable agricultural land reverted to bush, but the people of historic missions such as Mgwali, near Stutterheim, refused to move and several of the newly expropriated lands became inadequately serviced dumping grounds for forcibly removed "surplus people." Dimbaza, near King William's Town, became especially notorious after the documentary film *Last Grave at Dimbaza* raised an international outcry.

It was difficult enough to find credible traditional leaders in this new Ciskei, but it was even more difficult to create a Ciskeian political identity as opposed to a

Transkeian political identity, since Matanzima of Transkei had argued, reasonably enough, that, since all the people on both sides of the Kei were Xhosa, the logic of ethnicity demanded a single Xhosa state. Such a move, however, would have exposed East London, South Africa's tenth city, and the entire "white corridor" extending from East London to Queenstown in the far interior. Political considerations also dictated the exclusion of King William's Town, otherwise its obvious capital, from the future Ciskei state. By way of compensation for the loss of KWT, Ciskei President L L Sebe was given financial *carte blanche* to build a brand-new city at nearby Bhisho that would express "the life and spirit of the Ciskei people." The fake new capital of Ciskei dovetailed nicely with its President's fake doctorate, its fake industrial hub at Dimbaza, and its fake independence in December 1981. On the symbolic level, a fake new "national shrine" was erected on Ntaba kaNdoda, where Ciskei civil servants were compelled to gather every Easter on pain of losing their jobs. A pity really, because Ntaba kaNdoda was actually the site of the independent Xhosa's last stand during the Last Frontier War, and the subject of a famous poem by S E K Mqhayi (d. 1945), the Xhosa national poet. A monument aligned with the Eastern Cape historical experience might have stood forever. But, built as it was on the loose gravel of the Ciskei homeland, President Sebe's Ntaba kaNdoda crumbled along with his homeland.

The historic community of Kat River was another casualty of the misconceived Ciskei enterprise. Dispossessed by crooked lawyers in the early twentieth century, the few remaining community members took refuge at Tambookiesvlei, the private farm of Kat River Commandant Christiaan Groepe. Classified by the apartheid government as "coloureds," the Kat River people were not regarded as Ciskeians, and the majority of them were expropriated along with their white neighbours during the 1980s. A very few clung on to the venerable Dutch Reformed Church at Hertzog, adjacent to Tambookiesvlei, only to find – in the new South Africa – that Tambookiesvlei is also claimed by the descendants of the prophet Ntsikana (d. 1822), whose grave is located in its midst.

Bhisho is now the capital of the democratic province of the Eastern Cape. A community group is currently staging an annual festival at Ntaba kaNdoda. Retired Archbishop Ndungane has been tasked by the President with resuscitating Healdtown and other historic missions. But black and white people are still contesting Salem, black and coloured people are still contesting the Kat River. The pictures in this book vividly illustrate today's Eastern Cape, living uncertainly as it does among the fragments of its yesterdays. It does not seem as if we are ignoring these yesterdays, but nor does it seem as if we are utilising them to build afresh. Albert Einstein once said that "the distinction between past, present and future is only an illusion," and nowhere has this been more true than in the Eastern Cape.

— Jeff Peires

The road to Somerset East and Bruintjieshoogte and the Boschberg range. The 100 Years War between Colony and Xhosa (1779–1878) began in this region. The series of clashes historically known as Frontier Wars date back to 1779 when Xhosa people, Boers and the British clashed intermittently for nearly a century. These were largely due to colonial expansion which eventually dispossessed San, Khoikhoi and Xhosa people of their land and livestock, among other things.

The ruins of the historic Prinsloo farmstead. Willem Prinsloo was the first settler at Boschberg, later renamed Somerset East. The Dutch authorities held the Prinsloos responsible for *"violences and annoyances"* against the Xhosa, which resulted in the first Frontier War (1779).

Looking over Somerset East from the Boschberg.

Memorial at the top of the Zuurberg range to the Graaff-Reinet Landdrost, Anders Stockenström, who was killed by Xhosa warriors when they heard of the attacks of Colonel Graham in the Zuurveld, on 28 December 1811 while meeting a Xhosa delegation at the outset of the Fourth Frontier War. Stockenström was advising them to abandon their homes in the Zuurveld, immediately prior to Colonel John Graham's offensive to clear the Zuurveld of all its Xhosa inhabitants.

Doorn Nek, the pass where the memorial to Landdrost Anders Stockenström is situated,
Zuurberg.

Entrance to a game farm, one of many in the present district of Albany, formerly known as the Zuurveld.

KwaGompo (Cove Rock) from which the warrior prophet Makhanda Nxele (Makana) declared, in 1816, that he would summon Xhosa ancestors to rise from the sea to help drive whites from the land. East London.

A closer view of KwaGompo (Cove Rock). East London.

The Amalinde, site of the most terrible battle ever fought amongst the Xhosa themselves (October 1818). The army of King Hintsa, supported by Chief Ndlambe and led
by Makhanda Nxele (Makana) defeated the army of Chief Ngqika, scorned for his ambi-
tion, greed and collaboration with the British. Debe Nek, directly opposite present-day
Dimbaza between Fort Hare and King William's Town.

The Inxuba or Great Fish River in the region of Somerset East. It was this fertile land beyond the Zuurveld which lured settlers and caused the confrontation with the Xhosa, resulting in the 100 Years War of Resistance, or Frontier Wars.

Farmland in the Somerset East region close to the Great Fish River, or Inxuba River, as it is known to the Xhosa who fought nine Wars of Resistance over a period of exactly 100 years to keep their land, which they ultimately lost.

Van der Kemp's Church in Bethelsdorp, Port Elizabeth. Johannes Theodorus Van der Kemp, a Dutch medical doctor, was the first Christian missionary in the Eastern Cape sent out by the London Missionary Society. Arriving in 1799, he first settled at the Mgqakwebe (Pirie) River near Chief Ngqika's residence, but was expelled in 1800 by rebel Boers who suspected him of being a British agent. He then moved to Graaff-Reinet, but was again expelled by rebel Boers. He finally set up his mission station in Bethelsdorp, near Algoa Bay, in 1803 to mostly Khoi and released slaves.

View of Van der Kemp's Church in Bethelsdorp, Port Elizabeth.

Present day church service in Van der Kemp's Church in Bethelsdorp, Port Elizabeth.

Memorial, in the vicinity of Bruintjieshoogte and the Boschberg, to trekboers who left for the Transvaal and Natal in 1837.

Karel Landman memorial to the Afrikaner trekkers who departed from the Zuurveld for Natal and the Transvaal in 1837 to escape British rule. Landman farmed in this area and served briefly as commandant of the Natal trekkers, following the killing of Piet Retief by the Zulu King Dingane. Alexandria.

Port Elizabeth (Algoa Bay). The Pyramid erected by Sir Rufane Donkin in memory of his deceased wife Elizabeth. He renamed Algoa Bay, Port Elizabeth, in her honour. Donkin was Acting Governor when several groups of British colonists arrived and were settled by the British government and the Cape authorities in the Eastern Cape in 1820, so called the 1820 Settlers.

A history museum housed in one of the early buildings of Castle Hill, Algoa Bay, present-day Port Elizabeth.

Present-day city centre, Port Elizabeth.

Albany Museum with detail depicting the arrival of the 1820 Settlers. Grahamstown.

Monument to the 1820 Settlers, Grahamstown.

Place of Parting of the 1820 Settlers, 2 metre quartzite monolith, Assagai Bush. One of
the points from which 1820 Settlers were directed to their allotments. Albany/Zuurveld.

Monument marking the point at which 1820 Settlers crossed the Kowie River in present-day Port Alfred.

Southwell, one of the many centres in which 1820 Settlers were placed, and where my ancestor, Robert Newton Dunn settled, before leaving the Eastern Cape for Port Natal and present day Durban in 1834. Albany/Zuurveld.

Toposcope, from which point 1820 Settler farms were surveyed and families disbursed to
their various allotments.

St John's Anglican Church, Bathurst. The church was a sanctuary and refuge for settlers during the wars of 1834, 1846 and 1851.

Entrance to a game farm, Albany/Zuurveld.

Grahamstown Cathedral. According to current Ndlambe descendants, this was the site of
Ndlambe's Great Kraal. Grahamstown.

The first building in Grahamstown to be used as a jail in the 1820s. In 1824, it was converted into a school, and later a library.

Old Gaol in Grahamstown, built in 1823.

Old Gaol in Grahamstown, built in 1823.

The Great Fish (Inxuba) River mouth.

Bushmans River mouth and seaside village.

The Great Fish (Inxuba) River, Committees Drift. This natural border of the Cape Colony was hotly contested during the 100 Years War. Any Xhosa who crossed this divide after 1812 were liable to be shot on sight, a state of affairs that lasted until at least 1835, and at various times during flareups of violence during the many wars until 1879. After the Fifth Frontier War (1818-19), the Xhosa beyond the Fish River were evicted, and the territory between the Fish and Keiskamma Rivers (later the districts of Peddie and Alice) was proclaimed a "ceded territory" by Lord Charles Somerset.

The Great Fish (Inxuba) River in the region of Somerset East. This was the fertile land
beyond the Zuurveld that lured settlers and caused the confrontation with the Xhosa,
resulting in the 100 Years War of Resistance.

Agricultural museum and mural. Bathurst (named after Lord Bathurst, the British Colonial Secretary), was originally intended to be the centre of the 1820 Settlement. But most of the settlers soon abandoned their agricultural holdings and flocked to Grahamstown, the military (and therefore commercial) centre.

Salem Country Club. Salem (meaning peace), a settler village established in 1820 was the site of an incident during the Sixth Frontier War (1834-36) in which the unarmed Quaker, Richard Gush, persuaded the Xhosa warriors to withdraw after providing them with bread to appease their hunger. Subject of Guy Butler's play, *Richard Gush of Salem*, it was also the scene of a rape in J M Coetzee's novel *Disgrace*. The area is now the subject of a protracted land claim. Zuurveld/Albany.

St Andrews School began life as the "Kaffir College," the Anglican Church's equivalent of Healdtown (Methodist) and Lovedale (Presbyterian) schools. It was there that Rev Mullins taught black people to play rugby. Grahamstown's white residents were, however, not happy to have so many black scholars amongst them, and so, in 1904, it was relocated to St Matthews in the Keiskammahoek District. St Andrews College, Grahamstown.

Private game and nature reserve in Albany/Zuurveld.

Southwell Country Club and cricket pitch. One of the many areas in which 1820 Settlers were settled in the Zuurveld/Albany district.

Salem Anglican Church and cricket pitch.

Mduduzeli Mkele, Yonela Mcanda and Sima Mkele, on the rise overlooking Grahamstown from which Makandha Nxele (Makana) and his forces attacked the garrison in 1819.

Plaque commemorating an act of heroism by Elizabeth Salt, a Settler woman caught up in the Battle of Grahamstown in April 1819. Salt, a French woman married to an Englishman, took advantage of the fact that the Xhosa never harmed women and children, to retrieve a keg of gunpowder and bring it to soldiers in the barracks. The account on the plaque is of her making her way through a mass of warriors, which is likely a fanciful account of the event. Grahamstown.

Egazini Memorial to the more than 1000 warriors slain in the failed 1819 attack on Grahamstown led by Makhanda Nxele (Makana). Nxele surrendered months later and was sent by the British to be imprisoned on Robben Island. The contested site of Makana's Kop on the horizon, now with Reconstruction and Development houses forming part of the contemporary townships of Grahamstown.

The burial place of Ntsikana (1780–1821), a prophet of Ngqika. He was one of the first Xhosa to convert to Christianity, around 1815, and was rival to Makhanda Nxele. Ntsikana was also the first great Xhosa hymn-writer. Kat River Settlement.

Looking north towards the Amathole Mountains from Grahamstown. The Great Fish River
bush lies in the foreground.

Bridge over the Great Fish (Inxuba) River, built in 1877. The region of Committees Drift
was of great strategic value to the British because of its proximity to Grahamstown.

The rugged heights of the Amathole mountains, which served as a refuge and strategic vantage point for embattled Xhosa warriors.

The Great Fish (Inxuba) River, streaming through the Great Fish River Nature Reserve in which the bush served as a tactical retreat and formidable fortress for Xhosa militants.

The formidable Great Fish (Inxuba) River bush.

Looking out towards Fort Hare from the Amathole Mountains. It is from vantage points such as this that the Xhosa generals commanded their resistance against the British forces during the later wars.

The town of Fort Hare lies in the foreground, overshadowed by the Amathole Mountains..

Fort Hare University and site of the fort, the ruins of which still lie within the university grounds.

Great Fish River Nature Reserve, in which lies the Great Fish River bush, used so effectively by Xhosa warriors to wage their war in defense of their land.

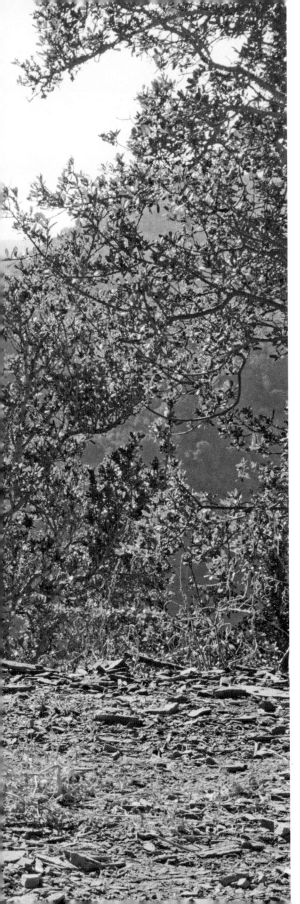

Tour guides Miranda Kakancu and Cebo Lekhanya Vaaltein (who passed away shortly after the making of this image) of Mbodla Eco-Heritage Tours at the Mankazana Cave where women and children were slaughtered by British forces in the 100 Years War. KwaNdlambe, Peddie.

British military graves, Fort Willshire, Keiskamma River, Keiskammahoek.

Barracks ruins, Fort Willshire, Keiskammahoek.

Fort Willshire was erected on the Keiskamma River by the British military during the Fifth Frontier War (1818–1819) and named after Colonel T Willshire. During the 1830s it served as a marketplace for trade. It was also Sir Benjamin D'Urban's base of operations during the Sixth Frontier War (1834–1835). Keiskamma River.

Signal tower, Fraser's Camp, close to the Great Fish (Inxuba) River and across the river from Peddie.

View from the ruins of a barracks occupied by the British, of the Mgwangqa battle field. Mhala, son of Ndlambe, led his forces against the British here in one of the many battles that comprised the 100 Years War of Resistance. Peddie.

Boma Pass lies submerged in the waters of Sandile Dam. It was here that King Sandile and his forces successfully attacked a British army convoy on 24 December 1850, marking the start of the Eighth Frontier War, also known as Mlanjeni's War, which lasted until 1853.

Theopolis, former garrison, then mission settlement, destroyed by the British Settlers when the mostly Khoi and free slave inhabitants were suspected of assisting in the Kat River Settlement rebellion of 1853. Between Southwell and Kasouga.

Theopolis, former garrison, then mission settlement, destroyed by the British settlers when the mostly Khoi and free slave inhabitants were suspected of assisting in the Kat River Settlement rebellion of 1853. Between Southwell and Kasouga.

The ruins of Theopolis.

Shards of pottery and debris from the ruins of
Theopolis, former garrison, then mission settlement, destroyed by the British settlers when
the mostly Khoi and free slave inhabitants were
suspected of assisting in the Kat River Settlement
rebellion of 1853. Between Southwell and Kasouga.

Fort Brown, Great Fish River.

Fort Armstrong on the Kat River. Originally known as Camp Adelaide, it was later named
Fort Armstrong after Captain A B Armstrong who was based there in 1835. The Fort
was garrisoned by the Cape Corps (Khoi) regiment, who surrendered the Fort to Willem
Uithaalder, Khoi General of the Kat River rebels, on 23 February 1851, during the the
Eighth Frontier War – so-called Mlanjeni's War. Balfour, Kat River Valley.

Fort Armstrong on the Kat River was declared a national monument in 1938. Kat River Valley.

Church elder, W Pringle, with silverware donated by a descendant of the founder of the
N G Kerk at Herzog, which was expropriated by the South African government circa 1980,
due to the consolidation of the Ciskei Homeland. Most of the church members left for a
place called Friemersheim, near Mossel Bay, purchased with the expropriation money.
Fewer than ten families remained behind, clinging to the old church. Tambookiesvlei, Kat
River Settlement.

Churchgoers, Tambookiesvlei, Kat River Settlement.

Tambookiesvlei, Kat River Settlement, where Khoi were settled by Sir Andries Stockenström after Maqoma was expelled in 1828, thus setting up tensions within these groups
that exist to this day.

Tambookiesvlei was the private farm of Commandant Christiaan Groepe of the Kat River. Most of the Kat River people retained their lands even after the 1850s rebellion, but were later tricked out of their land through a legal scam called the "Boedel Erven Act." The remnants of the community were thereafter allowed by the Groepe family to settle on their private farm.

Tambookiesvlei, Kat River Settlement.

Detail from the monument to the 'Great Cattle Killing' or 'Great Hunger,' which resulted from the visions of the prophetess Nonqgawuse, causing many Xhosa to destroy livestock and crops in 1856/57, resulting in a great famine and the destruction of the Xhosa economy. King William's Town.

The burial place of the prophetess Nongqawuse, whose vision was to cause the Xhosa to destroy their cattle and grain stores in the belief that their dead would arise and the world would be reborn anew – without settlers and colonialists. Alexandria, Albany/ Zuurveld.

Cattle-killing Monument. The memorial to the 'Great Cattle Killing' or 'Great Hunger' of the 100 Years War lies in the mass burial site and town cemetery. The monument was erected by the Eastern Cape government around 2008. In the aftermath of the Nongqawuse prophecies, starving people made their way to the colonial capital of King William's Town in the hope of getting food and medical care. Many of them died nevertheless, and their bodies were buried in the Edward Street Cemetery, adjacent to the graves of British soldiers killed in the wars. They were forgotten there for more than 100 years until their bones were uncovered by developers laying the foundations for a new townhouse complex. King William's Town.

Chief Mxolisi Hamilton Makinana, descendant of five warrior chiefs who fought against the Boers and British in the 100 Years War of Resistance to settler and colonial domination. Ndlambe Village, Great Fish River.

A village at the foothills of the Amathole Mountains from which the Xhosa generals defended their territory in the 100 Years War of Resistance to settler and colonial domination.

Memorial to the battle of 1819 in which Makhanda Nxele's forces attacked the garrison
of Grahamstown. Over a thousand warriors were slain in this battle, which the Xhosa lost.
Egazini, Grahamstown.

The fruits of dispossession: soil erosion due to over-crowding and over-grazing in KwaNdlambe Village, Peddie.

Southwell Country Club and cricket pitch. One of the many areas in which 1820 Settlers were settled in the Zuurveld/Albany district.

The ruins of the Dimbaza Border Industrial Park. Built in the 1970s as a source of cheap labour for industrialists (and ostensibly employment for Ciskei Homeland citizens). This industrial zone collapsed after 1994.

Moravian Mission Church, with what used to be a post office in the foreground. Enon, Zuurberg.

Moravian Mission Church and village school. This Moravian Mission settlement was founded in 1816 and the original church, with its yellowwood rafters, teak window frames and brass hanging lamps, built by the Enon villagers in 1821, is still in daily use. Enon, Zuurberg.

Moravian Mission village. Enon, Zuurberg.

Moravian Mission village. Enon, Zuurberg.

Peddie (Ngqushwa in Xhosa), frontier town and site of an important British garrison. It was also the settlement of Xhosa and Khoi loyal to the British regime. The town developed from a frontier post established in 1835, named Fort Peddie after Lieuteant-Colonel John Peddie. It became a municipality in 1905. Amathole District.

Fingo Village, Grahamstown (the Mfengu people or Fingo in the colonial lexicon). It was the intention of the apartheid government to move the Grahamstown township of Fingo Village to Committees Drift/Glenmore. But because the Fingo Village people had title deeds from Queen Victoria due to their service to the British military during the 100 Years War, this proved impossible.

Fingo Village, Grahamstown.

Winterberg Agricultural School with Fort Beaufort and the Winterberg in the background.

View of Healdtown mission and college, which now lies mostly in ruins. Fort Beaufort.

Gates of Healdtown mission and college, which now lies mostly in ruins. Fort Beaufort.

Ruins of a main building of Healdtown mission and college. Fort Beaufort.

Dilapidated outbuilding of Healdtown mission and college. Fort Beaufort.

Courtyard ruins of Healdtown mission and college. Fort Beaufort.

Balfour, Kat River Settlement.

Bhisho, built as the seat of the Ciskei homeland government, and now the capital of the
Eastern Cape Province. King William's Town.

Bhisho, built as the seat of the Ciskei homeland government, and now the capital of the
Eastern Cape Province. King William's Town.

View of Bhisho. King William's Town.

Ntaba kaNdoda, in the vicinity of Dimbaza township. Ntaba kaNdoda was named after the Khoisan Chief Ndoda, who lived on the mountain in the mid-1750s, and was killed in battle by the Xhosa King Rharhabe. It was also the site of the final battles of the 100 Years War. S E K Mqhayi, the Xhosa national poet, composed a famous poem praising the mountain. Since the fall of the Ciskei homeland, the site has fallen into disuse, though periodic attempts are made to rehabilitate it. Dimbaza, Debe Nek.

Ntaba kaNdoda Monument, Debe Nek.

The grave of Chief Maqoma (1798–1873) at the Ntaba kaNdoda Monument. Maqoma fought in the in the Sixth (1834–1836) and Eighth (1850–1853) Frontier Wars. The alleged bones of Maqoma, the most famous Xhosa warrior chief, were somehow found on Robben Island, and reburied in a Heroes Acre established at the Ntaba kaNdoda Monument, which was commissioned by Lennox Sebe of the Ciskei Bantustan government as a homage to the Xhosa Chiefs who fought the British. Ciskei civil servants were obliged to attend a Ciskei national religious civil service held on the Monument every Easter.

Ntaba kaNdoda seen from Debe Nek.

Ntaba kaNdoda. The battle of Amalinde was fought in this region.

The grave of Chief Maqoma (1798–1873), a Xhosa warrior who played a significant part in the Sixth (1834–1836) and Eighth (1850–1853) Frontier Wars, at Ntaba kaNdoda Monument, commissioned by Lennox Sebe of the Ciskei Bantustan government as a homage to the Xhosa Chiefs who fought the British.

Burial ground and memorial to Ngqika, Xhosa king and warrior. Burns Hill.

Maqoma's original Great Place in the Kat River Valley. He was removed in 1829 from this site by the British for a minor infringement, and Khoikhoi settled in his place by Commissioner-General Andries Stockenström in a move that would prove disastrous. Kat River Valley.

Sandile's grave in the Isidenge Forests of the Amathole mountains, about 16 kilometres from Stutterheim. Two British soldiers were buried in the same grave.

King William's Town, re-established in 1847 after the War of the Axe, was the administrative centre of British Kaffraria, and conceived as a colonial capital. At one point it was one of the biggest cities in southern Africa, but it declined after British Kaffraria was absorbed into the Cape Colony in 1866, and was overtaken by East London during the Anglo-Boer War.

Ginsberg, hometown of Steve Biko, and cradle of the Black Consciousness Movement.
King William's Town.

Graveyard in which 1970s struggle hero and Black Consciousness leader Steve Bantu Biko,
who died in police detention in 1977, is buried and memorialised. King William's Town.

Chief Mxolisi Hamilton Makinana, descendant of five warrior chiefs who fought against the Boers and British in the 100 Years War of Resistance to settler and colonial domination, standing with his councillor, Richard Jonya, at the Nyikinyawa Cliffs where his forefather mounted one of many attacks on the invading forces. Great Fish River.

The fruits of dispossession: soil erosion due to over-crowding and over-grazing in KwaNdlambe Village, Peddie.

Nolukhanyo township entrance, Bathurst.

AFTERWORD

Photographing in the Presence of Absence

Mahmoud Darwish's seminal narrative on exile, loss, and collective remembering, *In the Presence of Absence*, written as he was approaching his last years, is an elegy for a life spent in exile; here, childhood and youth, along with the olive and orange groves of Palestine, are also countries from which Darwish has been displaced – beautiful landscapes to which he could never return. Darwish and his family went into exile in 1948, when he was only seven years old; his memory of homeland is inevitably an amalgamation of other, older family members' memories and experiences of loss. For the exile, especially one who has little to no memory of what home constituted, ideas surrounding "home" become intertwined with the shame of expulsion, sorrow, and longing. And once one experiences expulsion, an unease follows one's efforts at making home. One may be able to return to the physical spaces that constituted home, as did Darwish, as a "present-absentee." But even though he was able to return to his family's lands – now located in Israel – to replenish his memory, he recognised the impossibility of "homing." His and his people's existence there was, and is being, systematically obliterated; their customs, food, the lands they cultivated, and the buildings in which they were born and raised taken over and re-presented on the world's stage as another people's rightful heritage.

But Darwish's writing is more than a reflection of personal pain. He also chronicles defining historical moments and political decisions that helped shape the experience of being Palestinian: he chronicles the 1948 Nakba and the Deir Yassan massacres, the 1979 Sabra and Shatila refugee camp massacres in Beirut, as well as later disappointments, such as the failed Oslo Accords. Darwish records the effects of each of these unbearable disappointments and violent ruptures, driven, undoubtedly, by a personal imperative. His meticulous record-keeping indicates that he is equally driven by a political imperative. He writes against systematic efforts to erase traces of his people's existence, and to remind us of the long political battle to maintain, in active memory, his people's right to occupied landscapes. He writes despite the violence of occupiers who intend to remove physical bodies of Palestinians out of their landscapes and to demoralise the population into an acquiescent acceptance of exile.

Whilst Mahmoud Darwish and countless other Palestinians from younger generations have recorded a tapestry of living memories about their homeland and disseminated stories about a flourishing culture of resistance, what happens when the record of one's people's existence, of one's sustained fight to remain on one's ancestral homeland has been all but forgotten? In the absence of recorded narratives, can photography step in to reveal trauma – consisting of a network of environmental, social, and economic fractures – in a colonised landscape, centuries after traumatic wars leading to one's displacement? Is it possible for photographs to return that which is outside the frameworks of our present thinking – an elusive, disappeared body of remembrances – into focus, calling on us, the audience, to begin a conversation with those silenced narratives? Cedric Nunn's photographs in *Unsettled: The 100 Years War of Resistance by Xhosa Against Boer and British* is such an attempt – an invocation of exiled, silent, and silenced memory, and a call to converse with a history we are not meant to remember. Nunn, as the photographer, "becomes the narrator, generating and validating a collective memory" (in Ana Tostões and Ana Maria Braga's words) though it is largely absent or erased from official history.

Photography is often associated with a "strong documentary value," and is used to create archives of a people's civilisation, especially when the structures they built are in danger of loss; photographs "can validate these objects as something worth preserving" and thus validate their creators' and builders' civilisation (Tostões and Braga). Moreover, photographs – even more so than narratives of personal experience – can, Susan Sontag noted in *On Photography*, "furnish evidence," providing a material body of evidence of things "we hear about but doubt." But because Nunn embarked on a project that seeks to represent and investigate, as Elliot Ross put it, "a long history characterised by erasure, silence, and defeat," the use of photography — a medium that is associated with presenting "the single moment, only derivable from the present" – seems, at first, to be unfeasible. The madness of his project is even more evident when one considers the fact that there are no monumental structures or physical bodies of evidence – things that audiences trained in the western tradition are taught to identify of as valid remainders of civilisation – to index and authenticate the existence of the Xhosa civilisation.

The central questions that Nunn's project raise include whether photographs are able to raise up history that is "not there but there" to the surface of our collective consciousness, especially when there has been a concentrated effort to suppress that history. What does a photographer do, in the absence of this material evidence – without a built environment that disturbs and/or damages natural landscapes – to provide the "evidence" we are so well-trained to look for as proof of a people's worth? Moreover, given that traditional modes of witnessing or confessing often leave "witnesses" or confessors feeling as though their testimonies and experiences have been appropriated and consumed by those who come into their communities to "collect" memories, is it possible for Nunn's work to disrupt those violent and violating modes of documentation? Can these photographs begin to point us towards a more ethical mode of witnessing, challenging audiences to take up the long labour of reflecting upon a silenced history? We realise, as we reflect on Nunn's photographs, that what we are called on to do, as an audience, is to engage with the unreadable, unrepresentable, and, ultimately, the unassimilatable in South Africa's history, given the political frameworks that were set up to paint the colonial powers as unquestionably superior. That means that audiences, much like the photographer, must enter this conversation whilst being preoccupied with the difficulties and impossibilities of representing a history is that has been actively "disappeared," but has, nonetheless, real, material effects on the present lives of those who live in the presence of those absences (Ross).

Nunn says that his work "is an invitation, really, for the viewer to imagine that history and time. To revisit the deed and recall the acts." *Unsettled* is an attempt to allow that traumatic history manifest itself, and make itself visible. We, as readers of these photographs, realise that the impetus is on us, the audience, to take on that labour, to synthesise new modes of detection as we create new narratives for this landscape; we realise that we must shift our focus from the familiar and call attention to things that are not present in the photographs – absences that, before, we never questioned.

In *The Disciplinary Frame*, John Tagg notes that the "discursive event" surrounding any colonisation and conquest is from "its inception . . . imbricated in power and bound to the generation of power." Our image repertoires of conqueror and conquered are determined by "performative rules invested in institutions, techniques, practices, and modes of behaviour," which, together, reinforce the ideologies and realities in which we have invested over multiple generations. Tagg argues, further, that the "performative arena" of discourse production is shaped by unspoken "rules of exclusion, limitation, and employment." Because they are unarticulated, we rarely question the frameworks that uphold accepted discourses of power; and because of our collective silence, they remain powerful. Together, the rules that determine our dominant worldviews and the silences that surround these powerful discourses operate "as forms of instigative violence – a violence that produces the event of meaning and impinges on the body, making it subject, constituting the subject that is subject to discourse." Though unacknowledged, such exclusionary, limiting, and violent epistemologies are intergenerational; our worldviews, hand-me-downs from our teachers, parents, and political leaders – each of whom absorbed the narrative of the vanquished, and each of whom were themselves "impinged" upon and subjugated by the restrictive discourses of colonial and apartheid violence – help frame our historical, political, socio-economic, and more recently, corporate values and structures.

Tagg points out, however, that "Panopticon and disciplinarity," whilst part of "concerted effects of specific material apparatuses and techniques . . . do not describe a remorseless and exhaustive system" or "a totalizing concept." He notes, moreover, "where its mechanisms were put into effect, its workings were never inexorable. The bodies it harnessed could never be entirely made subject to or subdued beneath its performative demands. It was actively resisted and undermined by counterpowers, evasions, and perverse reinvestments."

Given that the elements that are invisible in documentary photography, constituting what the photographer and writer Asim Rafiqui calls the "politics of the photograph" – the colluding silences surrounding photographs, as well as the political "manipulations that [silence] enforces" – remain outside the frame of the photograph, what possibilities do Nunn's photographs and the brief narratives he includes with each photograph offer us as we explore pathways out of limiting and limited colonial epistemologies? Given that the same technologies helped produce dominant discourses, what release might photography and narrative, positioned as each other's complementing unconscious, give us from the instigative violence that aided the colonial project of subjugation and erasure?

Nunn reminds us that he did not go to the Eastern Cape with a blank slate; he, too, had absorbed a powerful narrative – a narrative engineered by conquerors – informing him. When he thought of the Transkei, he imagined an "idyllic place" with rolling hills. However, the Eastern Cape, in the South African imaginary, is also "a failed State," and before he began his project five years prior, he, too, thought of it as "a dysfunctional place" with "potholed roads." But as he read more, Nunn learned, through the writings of early global travellers who visited the Eastern Cape in the 1400s and 1500s. Their descriptions of the Xhosa people painted them "as almost a perfect people, perfect in every sense, in their physique, in their speech, in their social relations, in how they organized their society, in their legal system." Whilst fashioning the non-threatening "other" as a "noble savage" is a common trope in colonial travellers' diaries, these descriptions of the Xhosa's remarkable hospitality and system of governance stands in stark contrast to what Nunn describes as current views. Nunn hastens to add that though there was some truth behind the stereotypes he carried with him, and that "corruption is endemic in the society," he began to wonder when and how "that shift" – from being a "noble" people who governed themselves admirably to being a "corrupt and dysfunctional" people – happened.

Nunn had also read Noel Mostert's book, *Frontiers: The Epic of South Africa's Creation and the Tragedy of the Xhosa People*, in order to prepare for this project. He credits Mostert's groundbreaking historical work for helping him better understand South Africa's seminal moment in global history. In *Frontiers*, he read about the Xhosa's extraordinary resistance, set against a backdrop of convergences: indigenous Khoi and San met migratory groups of Africans who were moving southwards and westwards into the space of the Eastern Cape. Then came Europeans, who arrived in the same region at a later date. The conquest of this region, strategically, geopolitically, was of global significance; Nunn notes that it could be compared to contemporary wars taking place in contested spaces of the Middle East and Asia, the Ukraine or

Syria today. As historians like Mostert point out, when the British annexed the Cape as a refuelling station for their ships, they had no intention of going much further into what was considered frontier territory. But as the trade routes to India, Indonesia, and China became more contested between the Portuguese, the Dutch, the Spanish and the French, the British realised that in order to control the port, they also had to conquer lands further and further into the Eastern Cape region.

The result of that fateful convergence on the "frontier," between the British and the Xhosa, was South Africa's 100 Years War. Although the more famous battle recorded in South Africa's history books is that which took place between the British and the Zulu, Nunn maintains, the conquest of the Xhosa – and the virtual destruction of customs ensuring their intergenerational, intimate relationship with the landscape of the Eastern Cape, each other, and their vast herds of cattle, which constituted the bedrock of their economy – "was crucial to the domination of the entire country." Nunn argues that learning about the brutality and the duration of this war is essential for understanding modern South Africa's complexities: "I would go so far as to say that it is not possible to understand our modern day social and political environment without bringing these events into consideration."

This conquest was no easy win for the British; to begin with, it took one hundred years to achieve that destruction. Yet, Nunn argues, championing the mythology surrounding the mighty Zulu – although it took the British army "less than six months" to destroy Shaka's resistance – is, in fact, essential to the systematic erasure and "organized forgetting" that helps erase the memory of "this extra-ordinary historic resistance" by the Xhosa.

The monumental history of British conquest and victory replaced the Xhosa's collective memory of their one-hundred-year battle against erasure, expunging their long and valiant struggle from the record. Nunn explains why this erasure is so significant to our present-day mind-sets: "The South African ruling regime has largely been affected by the success of the re-writing of our histories, after all most of them were educated in the western tradition where these myths were propagated. Not really believing in ourselves, we seem not to take seriously who we are or once were."

Unsettled gives us many views of rolling vistas and extraordinary landscapes; they are beautiful in that way that only the open landscapes of Southern Africa can be. There is little trace of a long and bloody resistance evident in these photographs. For instance, when we see images of farmland in the Somerset East region, especially those that are close to the Great Fish River the only hint we have of subsumed history is when Nunn reminds us this same river is known as "Inxuba River" to the Xhosa who fought a 100 Years War or Frontier War of resistance to keep their land. We learn that it was the land beyond this river that "lured settlers" and began the confrontation with the Xhosa, leading to this interminable war. What remains is the memory of the river's Xhosa name, a name that the descendants of the British who now own those vast tracts of land have deemed as "unpronounceable," and therefore not worthy of including in present-day cartographies. It is in such seemingly benign decisions – decisions centred around re-naming, or deeming whether something of the conquered other is picturesque or palatable enough to appropriate as one's own – that erasures and violent excisions take place.

Yet, these landscapes were the locations at which a series of South Africa's bloodiest battles between the newly arrived British colonialists and the Xhosa were fought. A nondescript roadway, titled simply, "The road to Somerset East and Bruintjieshoogte and the Bosberg range" (page 1) is situated in the region where the Hundred Years War began in 1789. We learn that this region was "shared by Boer and Xhosa until conflicts over land use spilled over into violence," and that the "ruins of the historic Prinsloo farmstead in Somerset East" (page 2) were once the home of the family "notoriously accredited with having been the trigger for the confrontation" that led to this great frontier war. Nunn reveals another beautiful vista (page 39), the location of a violent battle, and a subsequent forced removal: "After the Fifth Frontier War (1818–9), the Xhosa beyond the Fish were evicted, and the territory between the Fish and the Keiskamma (later the districts of Peddie and Alice) was proclaimed a 'ceded territory' by Lord Charles Somerset." Into these territories moved British settlers. The Zuurveld and Albany districts, won through conquest and forced removals, are now home to vast farms, private game lodges, and nature reserves.

Photographs of small-town squares, small-town idylls mask locations of violent erasure: the spire of a typical English-style church – grandly called the Grahamstown Cathedral – overlooks Grahamstown's quiet central square (page 33). Nunn's caption informs us that this was the "site of Ndlambe's Great Kraal, according to the current Ndlambe descendants." No trace of that kraal is to be seen, and no plaque reminds us of what was paved over in order for this English present to claim its presence.

Other photographs focus on slave settlements, emphasising that built structures in adjacent images were constructed using slave labour. The "Toposcope" in Bathurst – a large mound of stones set on a circular platform, surrounded by a low, protective stone wall and a view of a vast landscape of valleys beyond it – was the point from which "1820 Settler farms were surveyed and families disbursed to their various allotments" (page 29). The entrance to Albany Museum, with reliefs consisting of four heraldry flags and a sailing ship commemorates the arrival of the 1820 Settlers (page 23). A "Monument to the 1820 Settlers" (page 24) in Grahamstown consists of a sturdy woman, man and their children, all in European dress. The woman is completely covered by a long-sleeved dress made of thick fabric a bonnet that shadows her face; the man's body is hidden under an overcoat, his head topped by a top hat. Surrounding the monument are large aloe plants, some of which are flowering.

Whilst the monuments, statues, and plaques in the photographs are meant to validate the victorious British and the robust Afrikaner, what Nunn's photographs reveal are the violent erasures, the displacements, and hidden labour necessary for building generations of settler wealth.

Some of the built structures of the British speak not of victory or permanence, but of the insecurity of the conqueror. Nunn's captions tell us that St John's Anglican Church, Bathurst (pages 31–32) "was a sanctuary and refuge for settlers during the wars of 1834, 1846 and 1851." We realise the irony of constructing such safe houses: though the most trusty monuments of European civilisation – churches, cricket grounds, jails – were built to mark arrival, settlement, and permanence, the Xhosa were not in agreement with such arrogance.

Whilst there are memorials to slain Xhosa, like the Egazini Memorial to warriors slain in the 1819 attack on Grahamstown led by Makhanda/Nxele (page 51), most are in a poor state of repair, and are rarely visited and little known. Other sites have been subsumed entirely by the erasing hand of "development": the contested site of Makana's Kop on the horizon has been razed to welcome new Reconstruction and Development houses intended for the black residents of the area who, under apartheid, were not permitted into the city without a *dompass* (a passbook intended to regulate movement of black Africans in urban areas). These houses form part of the contemporary landscapes of Grahamstown: a benign face of development that still segregates poor black residents from white.

Other significant sites of Xhosa victories are quite literally drowned out of sight: it was only on Nunn's third visit that he found Boma Pass, located in the Keiskamma Hoek region (page 71). Boma Pass is the location at which "King Sandile and his forces successfully attacked a British army convoy on 24 December 1850, marking the start of the Eighth Frontier War [of the nine Frontier Wars], also known as Mlanjeni's war, which lasted until 1853." But the site of that battle now lies submerged in the body of water beyond Sandile Dam. Perhaps it was too threatening to maintain the memory of King Sandile's strategic success – this, despite having none of the British's army's famously advanced gunpowder and weaponry. Many other historical sites, like Boma Pass, are poorly signposted and were difficult to find. Typically, Nunn would see a signpost on the highway, indicating a particular location that hinted at an important event that he had heard of, "and then nothing else." So he would have to go blindly into the surrounding landscape, and try to imagine that the significant event may have taken place on a random hillside. Although he knew that there must be people who still have passed-down memory about the topography in which these battles took place, he rarely had enough time to attempt to find people in each region who would know where a specific battle unfolded, or where people were forcibly moved to after a defeat. Another such poorly signposted location was the site of the Gwadana Battle, which he learned was located not far from Umthatha. Through many conversations, he did find the exact location of the Gwadana Battle. But his trials show us that for the ordinary inhabitant of this landscape, no matter how connected she or he is to this geography, there is little connection with the memory of resistance. All that remains are shadows and hints, maintained in the memory of a few.

What does it do to a population to live in the "there-but-not-there" of a violent aftermath, which continues to have a deep impact on their day-to-day lives?

The experiences of historical displacements, together with the more contemporary violence of apartheid (which compounded the losses resulting from the 100 Years War on the Eastern Cape) manifest themselves as on-going traumas on the geographical landscapes and the bodies and psyches of people. Katherine Baxter argues that "infrastructural systems such as apartheid" that expose populations to "long-term endurance of racial segregation or long-term exposure to the threat of abuse" are even more insidious now, in the so-called "post-apartheid" era, because the cause of continuing violence is unseen, and often denied. That invisibility of the cause, and the denial of the cause make "the experience of trauma more severe." And because the cause of the trauma is unseen and difficult to pinpoint, those bearing the brunt of that historical (and ever-present) violence "are perceived as overreacting or responding in an unreasonable way" or are belittled. The resulting reaction to invisible traumas that are unacknowledged, but remain damaging can lead to a "'traumatic worldview,' which perceives the world suspiciously as operating 'in ways of which we have no knowledge and over which we have no control.'" Baxter reminds us that this returns us to Fanon, and his theorisations about the sources of internalised racism, described in *Black Faces, White Masks*. That first awareness of trauma, as Fanon noted,

> results in self-alienation: a distrust of the self, caused by a disjunction between external and internal experience. Such self-alienation, which unsettles the stable self-image of the traumatized subject, comes to operate like an invisible threat, in that its source is no longer identifiable. Both act in undetectable ways to inflict a trauma of anxiety on an individual's sense of self-identity.

As he began his exploratory trips to the Eastern Cape, Nunn realised that the Xhosa were resettled into "these vast reserves that are denuded, literally, of top-soil." They are overcrowded in these spaces and unable to continue the practices that allowed them to flourish there before the losses of the 100 Years War. Still, he notes that when he did actually encounter the Xhosa of the Eastern Cape – rather than have powerful narratives that aided colonial conquest inform him – he saw "an echo in them of the people that were described four hundred years ago, that grace is within them . . . you don't find litter, you find proud people who are generous and welcoming, and full of the irony of their predicament, but not necessarily broken or gripped by hate or all those negative things that can destroy a person, they've managed to overcome that and managed to see things in a very long perspective, very long vision."

That "long vision" is what we see in Nunn's work.

As we go though Nunn's photographs, we realise that this is a ravaged kingdom. Yet, although present-day Xhosas may be disoriented by long-term effects of conquest, their memory of nation, history, and custom are still intact in the most unassuming places, and carried faithfully by the most unlikely people. We see that the descendants of warriors and kings are now employed as guides who can take us into this mute theatre of war; Chief Mxolisi Hamilton Makinana, "descendant of five warrior chiefs who fought against the Boers and British in the 100 Years War of Resistance to settler and colonial domination" is pictured by the Great Fish River, Eastern Cape, with "his councillor Richard Jonya at the Nyikinyawa Cliffs where his forefather mounted one of many attacks on the invading forces" (page 133). And in KwaNdlambe, Peddie, Eastern Cape, "Tour guides Miranda Kakancu and Cebo Lekhanya Vaaltein of Mbodla Eco-Heritage Tours" rest at the mouth of Mankazana Cave, "where women and children were slaughtered by British forces in the 100 Years War" (pages 64–65).

They carry with them the narrative of defeat, but also the memory of resistance.

The haunting quality of the absences in Nunn's work help audiences begin a conversation with a value system deeply embedded in reifying colonial mythologies about the invader's military, political, and cultural superiority. Traces of subsumed history about this war, once brought into the frame of our thought processes, help us question powerful epistemologies – knowledge frameworks that celebrate and continue mythologies about the inherent superiority of European civilisation and military know-how that we believe led to the conquest of the vast landscapes of the Eastern Cape.

An occupier is well-served when there is no record of life left by those whose geographic, cultural, and symbolic spaces were taken over. Darwish's writing reminds and exhorts his fellow exiles: if they resign themselves to silence, "Who will tell our story? We, who walk upon this night, driven out of place and myth." His elegy to his memory of Palestine is an action, marking not the end of a struggle, but a victorious call inviting a response. Hearing his call, we resonate with memory. We return – symbolically, psychologically, and politically to the location of the struggle – by singing ourselves back through the narrative pathways he opens up. We re-locate ourselves there, in places in which we have been told we do not belong. There, we find our way back to being.

Like Darwish's poetry, Nunn's photographs do not produce easy lessons; these photographs are not "teachable moments" with a didactic narrative. Instead, he coaxes memory out of landscapes meant to maintain a strict code of silence. At times, he makes it sing – and what we hear, when we put our ear to this ground and listen to his photographs, is a dirge. These photographs sing to remember. They cannot recreate a history exactly – there is no recovering that body, buried deep through a well-engineered programme of forgetting. But in the snatches of song we hear from Nunn's seemingly nondescript landscapes, we learn of a valiant, one-hundred-year battle to retain a beloved land. So deeply buried is the memory of the relationship that the Xhosa of the Eastern Cape with these thorny landscapes, these craggy passes, these rolling grazing lands that we can only imagine the passion with which they fought to maintain a continued relationship with it. To look at these photographs is to learn that history, but also to understand how deftly it was erased. It is gone but still present; absent, yet still singing.

— M. Neelika Jayawardane

FROM THE PHOTOGRAPHER

As you can imagine, photographing an event as momentous as a 100-year-long war needs a lot of travel just to get to all the places that were implicated in it.

The idea came to me in a flash – as these ideas sometimes do; I was opening a show in Berlin, and I had the honor of having Makhenkesi Stofile, South African Ambassador to Germany, open the show.

In my chat to him afterwards I realized how little I knew of the Eastern Cape generally, and it dawned on me that there had been this incredible conflict that had shaped this region, and in fact South Africa, fundamentally. The idea excited me. As a photographer, there are many ideas that you're confronted with, but one that actually enlivens you is rare. And this idea stayed with me. I almost like to think that I responded to an ancestor's calling – I have those feelings about this project – I just met incredible people that guided this project and made it possible.

So I began to think and read and find as much information as I could, because I really knew nothing about the 100-Years-War period, and I knew very little about the Eastern Cape. As a photographer with thirty years' experience, the Eastern Cape had always eluded me somehow. I had spent very little time working in this region. Although I had been there and done some work there, it was not enough to get a grip on the province. I lived in Johannesburg for many years, and am now based in Durban, but I originate from KwaZulu-Natal. I had my ideas about what the Eastern Cape was about. Whenever I thought about the Eastern Cape, I thought about a failed state: a dysfunctional place with potholed roads. I had these pictures of the Transkei – rolling hills, idyllic beaches, crime, fishing, hippies hanging out in Port St John's. That was my picture of the Eastern Cape. When I moved back to KwaZulu-Natal in 2007, after 25 years in Johannesburg, I moved to a place that was fairly close to the border of the Eastern Cape, and I decided I wanted to engage with this province. This project has been an extraordinary way to encounter it.

My very first choice of an author to write an essay for this book would have been Uruguayan journalist, novelist and activist, the late Eduardo Galeano. Famous for his writings on South America, he was particularly noted for his insights on the perspective of memory, and remembering and imagining our origins and history and our passage in time – his project was about building historical memory against the 'desert of organized forgetting'. That resonated for me, because, for me, that's what the 'Frontier War' was. Apart from some specialists, South Africans have largely forgotten it. And I have to wonder if perhaps that has been a kind of organized forgetting, in the way that we don't particularly remember or acknowledge this extraordinary historic resistance, especially by the Xhosa, that took place over that period.

I located my project around the idea of *resistance*, rather than a frontier clash, which it was in some ways. (It was of course also a frontier clash.) I gleaned a huge amount of information from Noel Mostert's extraordinary tome, *Frontiers*, where he explains the developments in that region, speaking about the fact that there were indigenous people living in the Eastern Cape, and then the migration of Africans who moved into this space, which was then followed by Europeans also arriving there somewhat later; and then this extraordinary clash of civilizations that happened there. Mostert locates this clash as a significant global moment, in the sense that for the process that was taking place post-enlightenment and post-industrialization, the conquest of this region, strategically and geopolitically, was of great significance – perhaps similar to more contemporary moments that are taking place in parts of the Middle East and Asia today, where incredibly significant spaces like the Ukraine, Syria, or Iraq – contested spaces – are being grappled over.

My understanding of what took place in the Eastern Cape was about the need to control this region. Progressively, as things unfolded, when the British annexed the Cape, they initially had no intention of going much further than that, at that point in time. There was a lot of contestation in the British foreign office though – for many a great reluctance to engage any further than the Cape, particularly the Western Cape, which was their refueling station. Yet, as the trade route became more contested between the Portuguese, the Dutch, the Spanish and the French, there was an increasing need to control it so that the British would not be denied access to it. And when the British had managed to achieve that, they began to realize that in order to keep control of it, they needed to conquer further. So that was the premise of beginning to understand the need to conquer what the British regarded as a fractious region. In fact, there were some people who were quite eager to reach a negotiated settlement around the control of the Cape; but perhaps the hawks won the day in the foreign office, and ultimately a decision was made for the military to go out and play in the Eastern Cape, with disastrous consequences.

So, how do you photograph a conflict that took place a long, long time ago?

It obviously isn't easy; what became really apparent to me was that I would have to engage the landscape – and I'm not a landscape photographer per se. While I have produced a lot of images and photographed land issues from the 1980s onwards, I haven't regarded myself as a landscape photographer, and so it was a huge challenge for me to engage with this history from that angle. But that seemed the obvious way to go for me, to engage this space as land that was contested, land that was the site of trauma, but land that was also beautiful, enticing, alluring.

As I traveled the length and breadth of the province I tried to imagine myself in that time. Something I discovered along the way is that, in fact, I have 1820 Settler heritage – so I tried to imagine my ancestors arriving in this place – what they would have seen and experienced. It's not that easy now to imagine it, though, because the landscape is significantly different. But aspects of it can be seen.

The indigenous people, whether it was the Khoikhoi or the Xhosa, had a different attitude towards land, a more spiritual sense that I think still exists even to this day; a sense of land as being not something that you own, but something that owns you. I tried to imagine a lot of that.

So a lot of this project is about *imagining*, my imagining.

I am not an historian; I'm not an academic. I'm someone who engages with things in a visual way. Thanks to a Mellon Foundation Senior Scholar Fellowship, [based at Rhodes University in Grahamstown], I was able to meet people who had done a lot of thinking and work around these issues and I was able to benefit from that work that had preceded me. While my idea wasn't an original one, and many other people have engaged the issues of this period, I'd like to think that as a visual person I have brought something 'other' – not something different, necessarily, but a project that sees and imagines this period in quite a condensed form.

There were many places that I engaged with, that I visited and photographed – as you can imagine, a period that spans that kind of time frame had me swept to and fro throughout the province. Places like the Great Fish, or Inxuba, River, which was a significant border and so a significant site, and which I photographed at various points. Closer to home is the Egazini Memorial, which I'm told will be relocated, and which has apparently been vandalized much more since I made this image. Southwell – a place one struggles to find, because if you blink you miss it! – which I discovered my ancestors had been settled in only after I had visited it. My ancestors, both the Biggars and the Dunns, left the Eastern Cape within thirteen or fifteen years of arriving there in the 1820s and moved to KwaZulu-Natal: they, like other 1820 Settlers, had paid passage to the British government to come to South Africa, only to realize that they had been sent into a war zone and were being used as pawns by the British. They ultimately packed up and left, and soon integrated with a seemingly far more ferocious tribe, the Zulus in Port Natal, now Durban. And I'm the product of that integration.

Then there was Theopolis, which is not signposted at all, and which the ancestors really had to work hard to help me locate. I went there with Professor Julie Wells, an historian at Rhodes, who had been there twenty years before, but who really had no clue as to how to get there again. Eventually we found the place, which is an extraordinary place to visit. There are only the ruins of the town that existed there from the 1820s until it was destroyed by 1820 Settlers and the British in 1853. It was destroyed because the people who inhabited that town – freed slaves and Khoikhoi – joined the Kat River Rebellion and rose up against the Colony, and paid a devastating price. Probably hundreds of thousands of people died during this conflict, and for me it dawned more and more the degree of the heroism of their resistance, that was eventually equally as tragic.

Mankazana Cave was another such place on the banks of the Great Fish River where the Ndlambe tribe had hidden their women and children, but whom the British ultimately massacred there. And then of course the Bosberg, where the original conflict began in 1779, where I visited the ruins of the Prinsloo farm – the Prinsloos being credited by historians for creating the first major conflict of the many that continued for a hundred years.

When you understand that Colonel John Graham's – after whom Grahamstown is named – offensive to 'clear' the Zuurveld (what is now Albany) of all its Xhosa inhabitants, was a kind of ethnic cleansing of its time, and that the 1820 Settlers were sent to inhabit the area as a buffer after the Xhosa had been forcibly removed, you see and engage with that area a bit differently now as you drive through the landscape.

I visited the Memorial to the Great Cattle Killing in King Williamstown, which is a sad indictment of how we memorialize things in this country. I tried not to cover too many battle sites, and I also tried not to photograph too many forts – even though this area has one of the highest concentrations of forts in the world, I'm told – which is further testimony to how formidable a foe the Xhosa were to the British.

And this is another thing that struck me as someone who is half Zulu and who grew up imbibing the myth of the Zulu warrior – the Zulu people having been as formidable as the Xhosa people before Shaka imposed his 'unification' onto the Zulu people, but which ultimately fractured them.

There were two ironies for me: the irony of the fact that I had tried to avoid photographing forts, and yet my first exhibition of this body of work found itself located in a fort (Fort Selwyn, which is now a museum). I see my exhibition there as having been a type of occupation of the fort: I invited the Inkosi (Chief) of the Ndlambe people to speak at the opening, and so this fort was suddenly full of its 'foe' – but in this instance as celebrants, celebrating the opening of the exhibition and their ongoing survival. The other irony for me is the idea of the heroic Zulu warrior: in 1879 when the Eastern Cape was considered defeated, it is recorded that the British loaded up all of their armaments and their troops and headed for Port Natal (now present-day

Durban), and within three months overpowered the Zulus, who are nevertheless still recorded heroically as formidable warriors in most historical accounts. That is also why Galeano's comment about organized forgetting gripped me: we were encouraged to imagine something different to what in fact actually happened. As historian Michael Parenti has eloquently asserted, up until very recently, history has always been written not just by the victors, but by the elite classes amongst them who manipulated how we understand history by eliminating any opposition to their favorably constructed perspectives.

This war had devastating consequences for the people who were mostly the victims. One of these consequences, that is not spoken of very often, is the divisions that exist to this day amongst the Xhosa people. The British were masters of divisionary tactics when engaging an enemy. One of the salient things I've come to understand is that a large part of the history that emerged from this period was written not only by the victors, but also by the collaborators with the victors. There was a substantial amount of collaboration by Xhosa people who sided with the British during this war, and who were the first missionary converts who were progressively schooled in Western education. They were the first products of the missionary schools, and who went on to occupy high state and provincial offices, with that legacy evident still today. But there have been and still are others who resisted and continue to resist to this day, and continued to be alienated. These divisions exist because these individuals don't have generations of having been scholars, they are not that visible in powerful governmental positions, and their networks are not as engaged in various aspects of society. One articulation of the legacy of this history, though, which won the day, is that of Western progress and the success of the mission schools in producing those new scholars and professionals that a modern state requires. But to this day there are still people who live in vast reserves – that are denuded, literally, of top-soil, that are overcrowded; but when I encounter them, I still see an echo in them of the people that were described four hundred years ago: proud people who are generous and welcoming, and full of the irony of their predicament, but not necessarily broken or gripped by hate or those negative things that can destroy a person. They've managed to overcome that and to see things in a very long perspective, with very long vision. The irony is that the ones who have collaborated and are sitting with the largesse, the spoils of that collaboration, and the powerful positions and the resources that brings, I get a sense that they pay a price for that to this day. It's the price of the easy resort to cronyism, to corruption, because that has been a part of that culture for a long, long time.

Somebody like Makhanda, who attacked Grahamstown in 1819, and who was in fact the first person to engage with the missionaries as an intellectual, as a philosopher, and as a statesperson for his people, who tried to engage with the English, and understand the spiritual underpinnings of their civilization, was seen, and has been maligned by the other side as having been fickle: first in that he engaged with Christianity, but then revealed himself to be the general of an attacking army. Indeed he was all of these things. The Xhosa people have been and still are very spiritual people, and many of them are in fact now Christians. Ntsikana, instead of Makhanda, has been presented in the histories as the first successful Christian convert, not necessarily for having been the ideal convert – for he adjusted the directives of the faith to suit himself and his own needs and desires – but because his descendants and followers remained in the Church, and so had access to printing presses and education, and it is their viewpoints that have remained intact to this day.

So these were the kind of things I encountered and engaged with in executing and producing this project.

Another thing that struck me as I began this project was that I realized that in fact the bigger story was that of the conquest of the Khoikhoi and the San. I'm pursuing a trilogy here, and my next project will focus on the dispossession and the re-emergence of the Khoikhoi and the San as a First Nation people, who technically were made to be non-people for more than a hundred years. The land restitution process, for instance, didn't include them at all. I see the means of engaging with this, not as an historical telling, but as the re-emergence of a people that are taking back the pride they have, and the sense of who they are as a people, and proudly reasserting their presence back into their country.

The third part of the trilogy will look at slavery, because slavery is the elephant in the room in South Africa. The dysfunctionality seen in so many of the ghettoes of the Cape, and many other places in the country, owes its legacy to that.

Unsettled is the first part of this trilogy, which looks not only backwards for the sake of recounting history, but does so for the sake of understanding where we find ourselves in our current history going forward. *Unsettled* is also a paean to those many forebears and ancestors who paid a heavy price in the defense of freedom, who have largely been forgotten in the depths of time, to whom we owe a deep gratitude and, in a sense, whose struggles need to be continued.

— Cedric Nunn

Looking out towards Grahamstown. A descendant of the warrior chiefs who led five of the nine wars in the 100 Years War of Resistance against the Afrikaner and British settlers. KwaNdlambe Village, Peddie.

ACKNOWLEDGMENTS

This project was originally inspired by a conversation with the Honorable South African Ambassador to Germany, Stofile Mkenkesi, for which I am grateful.

Inclusion by the Market Photo Workshop in the Social Landscapes project, a French–South African partnership, allowed for the project to kick off and was invaluable in ensuring that, as is so often the case, the idea was not still-born.

The Arles Photo Festival allowed for the first International manifestation of the project, and the feedback from that process was key in shaping the rest of the work.

For enabling a great leap forward, a special word of thanks goes to Professor Anthea Garman and the Rhodes University School of Journalism and Media Studies, who directed me to the Mellon Foundation and the Senior Scholarship Award, which made the bulk of the work possible.

Nkosi Makinini of Ndlambe Village and the Ndlambe people, and community historian and spokesman Mr Samuel Nogqala where instrumental in shaping my understanding of this saga from the perspective of the Xhosa people.

Professor Julie Wells of the Rhodes University History faculty gave invaluable advice, hours of consultation and background information, which was key to the project.

Grey de Villiers, retired Fort Hare historian, generously gave invaluable input and time in the early stages of the project, which helped shape my approach.

Jill Schoolman and the Pirogue Collective have been fantastic in their support of the work.

So were Indra Wussow and Wunfderhorn Afrika unstinting in their enthusiasm to publish the German edition.

Thanks to Dr Ralf Seippel and Delia Klask, Tobias Lehr and Sizakele Angel Khumalo of Seippel Gallery for their unwavering and enthusiastic support.

I am indebted to Tracy Murinik, my agent and partner, for her editing skills and moral support.

Thanks also to Dennis Da Silva and Andile Komanisi of Silvertone International for their great attention to detail and artistic interpretation to the scans and prints.

Then to my daughter Lara Nunn and her mom Lindy Scholtz for their great patience during my preoccupation and frequent absences, and their total support throughout the making of this work.